SUNSPOTS

by

W. Clifton Adams

including

Photographs
by
A. Rhae Adams

COLLECTOR'S EDITION

© Copyright 2006 by W. Clifton Adams
Printed in the United States
All photographs reproduced by permission.
All photographs © A. Rhae Adams 2006

All rights reserved by author

ISBN 1-58597-407-2
Library of Congress Control Number: 2006934002

4500 College Boulevard
Overland Park, Kansas 66211
888-888-7696
www.leatherspublishing.com

Nothing in this book is true....

Anyone unable to understand how a useful religion can be founded on lies will not understand this book either.

— *Kurt Vonnegut*
Cat's Cradle   1963

God's thinking is not our thinking. If we don't recognize that, we recognize little.   This book isn't intended to present truth. If any one person finds any truth in reading this book, then together, we have accomplished something special!

Certainly, I have never known any of the characters in this book. They came from fiction as far as I know. We can only believe that God created fiction as much as reality.

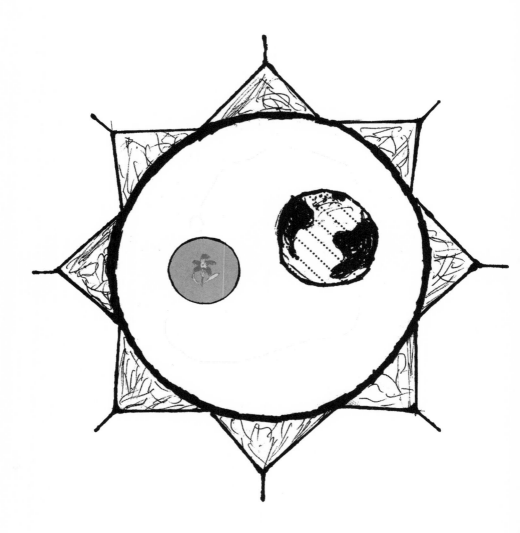

Dedication

Even before my mother died of cancer when I was fourteen, and certainly since, a few caring women provided the understanding and counsel that I needed so often.

It is to these, my personal Mother Moons, that this book is dedicated.

TABLE OF CONTENTS

Acknowledgements

James A. Michener told of a farmer driving nails into a fruit tree to explain his own renewed productivity following heart surgery in the mid-1980's. Perhaps that same analogy could apply to my finishing a version of this work after learning that I had a cancer in my colon and probably another one in my liver. That was in January of this year. Before that time, I had finished only two of the sunspots. I do appreciate all the competent attention I received from so many medical professionals during this period of my life.

The book would never have been finished without the constant love and support that I have received from Sara. We have been happily married for over 36 years. Since the early years, even before the thesis and the dissertation, she has been my advisor, critic and editor without whom nothing that I've written would ever have been fit for others to read. Yet, she has allowed me to put her name on little of what we have created.

Speaking of our creations: Our best, by far, has been Ami Rhae Adams. Rhae's willingness to augment my writing with her pictures guaranteed this would be a quality work.

My thanks, also, to many friends who have encouraged me to write over the years and helped me in so many ways toward that end. That list is too long for this space! Still, I do want to single out Doug Harris and Babs and Deems Brooks who have helped in so many ways, for so many years, including a proofing and comments on an early version of this book. For my other friends, please know that I remain grateful.

Thanks to the six readers who gave of their time to read and provide quotes for the dust cover.

Finally, thanks to Barbara Thomson and Michele Rook of Leathers Publishing who helped to make it the book you hold.

W. Clifton Adams
August 1, 2006

As a photographer, I hope that my pictures speak largely for themselves. That said, the photos in this book do not express my gratitude to the following: Clifton Adams, for conceiving and realizing this work, and providing a lifetime of support, love and open horizons; Sara Adams, for the same; Meghan and Jeff Nichols, and Doug Harris, for critique, advice and guidance; and above all, Rob Huang, for all.

Rhae Adams

Faith Moon

Once in a recent time, the man and the woman lived as one with themselves, with their animal friends and with nature. They had no need to toil because healthy food was easily within their reach as they frolicked among the rich vegetation with its beautiful flowers. They had no need for clothes because the climate was pleasant in their garden and they knew no shame.

Then, there came a time when an Evil One wandered by Earth and spied the man and the woman as they lounged peacefully by a babbling brook. This Evil One was agape.

"What is this that God has done?" The Evil One asked Himself. "This is definitely not proper! These creatures are modeled after God, but they know not the difference between good and evil. This cannot be! I must help them to distinguish between right and wrong. Surely God gave them free will."

Of course, the Evil One was correct because near where the man and woman rested was the tree of Forbidden Fruit. The Evil One had little difficulty convincing them that it was God's will that they should eat of this tree. He called it the Tree of Knowledge and told them that by eating thereof they would be one with God, like God.

As the Evil One knew, with the eating of the Forbidden Fruit, the paradise that the man and the woman had known, they knew no more. Henceforth, the Sun began continually to weep and the conditions on earth have been in constant flux ever since. Woman and Man have known struggle and strife.

However, when the Holy Essence saw what the Evil One had wrought, She said, "This is not correct! There must be balance. Where there is sorrow, some joy must emerge. Where there's suffering, there must be hope. Where there is ignorance, there must be sources of enlightenment. We must see that there are individuals who can provide insights to help people find that hope and feel that joy."

Faith Moon is one of those individuals.

George

Once on a modern time, George thought that he had it made. He had a lovely wife, two healthy and smart children who were almost out of college, a nice home that was almost paid for and a productive job that provided him security. He felt that he would live happily ever after.

Then, George's employer lost an established contract and George lost his job. George had many friends and was soon able to find another job; it just didn't pay as much money. George's wife had to convert from part time to full time so they could meet the children's tuition. So, George and his wife were able to spend less time together.

Indeed, George's new job was more demanding. It required of him frequent travel. He was unable to find time for any of the activities he had enjoyed over the years. Fairly quickly, he lost contact with his previous friends. Everything was changing so quickly and George did not like it.

He tried counting his blessings. At least he still had a job. He knew that there were people who could not find a job. Still, he was depressed. He became increasingly fearful of losing his current job. And, since he was no longer involved with his old friends, he couldn't count on them to help in finding yet another one.

On one of his business trips, he sat next to an ageless woman. He thought he was probably older than she was, but she projected an understanding gained from experiences exceeding his own. He learned her name was Faith Moon. Somehow the name fit her.

As they talked, he found himself telling her of his concerns, his cares. She seemed to understand. Eventually, she said:

Life is change. Change is life.
Accept the change occurring in your life,
And you can come to feel a higher rhythm.

Life's rhythm is not symmetrical.
It often does seem contradictory.
It's moving constantly in unpredictive ways.

The vee of the geese never is complete.
Some lone goose always struggles to move to the front,
While some lead goose anticipates being replaced.
Yet, from afar, the purpose served by their vee, we all see.

We generally cannot understand our purpose here.
Still, we may feel and move with nature's rhythm.
At times, this may require a focus on our acts not on our goal.

When George departed the plane, he resolved to focus more on what he was doing and to worry less about the future.

He saw both of his children graduated from college before he received a promotion. Yet, in the meantime, somehow he managed to find more time to spend with his wife and felt more in harmony with her once the children had left.

Mr. Thomas and Mr. O'Hare

Once on a modern time, Mr. Thomas and Mr. O' Hare were in competition. They had started grocery stores at the same time, across the street from each other. Well, to be exact, Mr. O'Hare started a butcher shop and Mr. Thomas started a vegetable stand. However, O'Hare quickly expanded his shop so that, before long, it offered a full line of merchandise. Thomas more slowly added to his offerings.

Soon, everyone agreed that it made more sense to shop at O'Hare's because it provided more one-stop shopping. However, they also agreed that they liked shopping with Thomas much more. Thomas was friendlier. He took time to visit with his customers, and, when times were difficult for one of them, he would grant additional time to pay the bill.

Generally, then, people did their regular shopping with O'Hare and visited with Thomas. O'Hare continued to expand, increasing his advantage in convenience. Thomas' business continued to dwindle.

Among Thomas' loyal customers was Faith Moon. When she was in his store one day, they were marveling at how quickly O'Hare had developed his store into a supermarket. Thomas expressed some concern about his decline in business to Mother Moon. She told him:

Do not overly concern yourself.
Life is not a sprint but a marathon.

Continue doing the things you do best.
Do them the best you can.
Yet highlight for others your qualities.

Lombardy poplar trees grow fast and tall,
But easily fall in the wind.
The dogwood tree grows slowly, small but stout.
Generations see its beauty last.

You are a dogwood tree.
Your future with great promise is full.
But wait no longer your flowers to display.

Promote the assets that are yours
And you will prosper with slow growth even.

You need to pace yourself and be content
Your fresh produce brings pleasure to others and you bring
*   them joy.*

Blessed be you for making these things premiums in your life!

Thomas did begin running specials on his best produce and introduced double values on coupons. His business increased sufficiently that he had no worries of bankruptcy.

O'Hare continued to expand. He felt content that he had won the race with Thomas. O'Hare hired a manager and bought a condo in Florida. Unfortunately, the manager had no head for business and the store had become too large for its market, especially when the new supermarket opened across town.

Mrs. Shue

Once on a modern time, there was a woman named Mrs. Shue. She had four young children. She did not know what she would do. Her house was like a den. Her husband's pay, on which they could depend, did not cover all that she had to spend. Then one day, like out of the blue, an idea came to Mrs. Shue.

The Shue Day Care Center, over the years, grew to be one of the most successful businesses in all the town. The Shue children, one by one, went from being playmates with the charges who spent their days under the care of Mrs. Shue to themselves being care providers and supervisors of the activities of the kids.

As her children grew, so did the facilities. The Shue Day Care Center evolved into a multi-room complex in a shopping center on the main street in town.

As her children accepted increasing responsibility for the running of the center, Mrs. Shue's attention turned away from providing for her family and, thus, away from the center. With the center doing so well, she saw no further need to be involved with its day-to-day operation.

First one and then another of her children finished high school and went away to college. Of course, with two workers gone from the center, the services suffered. As the services suffered, parents began finding other placements for their children. Then, the third Shue child left for college.

Income from the center went down, expenses for the education of the Shue children increased. Again, Mrs. Shue did not know what to do. Out of frustration, Mrs. Shue sought the advice of Mother Moon. After listening to Mrs. Shue, Faith Moon smiled and said:

As you do know from years ago,
If you want something to occur
The effort must come initially from you.

Remember nothing works unless you do.
Everything works for good when you do.

Before, you worked like a bee
Providing for your hive.
But then you acted like the queen expecting others to care for you.

Now, you must work again.
But this time, be like the dolphins in the sea
Who are as one with their environment.

Enjoy your work because it is a part of you.
You are a vessel full of care.
If you make gifts of your own energy
You will again find happiness.

Mrs. Shue saw truth in what Mother Moon told her and returned to the daily running of her center. Two of her children became teachers, one a writer of children's books and the youngest developed into a fine actor.

Cindy

Once on a modern time, Cindy's parents were killed in a tragic car accident. Cindy was fifteen at the time. She was sent back to town to live with her father's sister.

Cindy's parents left her a considerable trust, but she couldn't receive the money until she graduated from college. The fund guaranteed her education but otherwise gave control of the funds to Cindy's aunt.

Cindy's aunt was widowed with two teenaged daughters who were slightly older than Cindy. The aunt had an income provided by her late husband's insurance, but she did welcome the additional money provided by Cindy's estate.

It wasn't long before the aunt started thinking of this extra money as being hers. She saw no need to waste it on her niece, especially when her own needs and those of her daughters were so great. In all likelihood, Cindy wouldn't even go to college, she thought, especially if she wasn't encouraged to do so.

Over the next two years, the wardrobes of the daughters grew in splendor while Cindy's dwindled. Cindy's requests for new clothes were met with the dresses discarded by her cousins. Those dresses, she was able to alter down to her size; so, she contented herself. After all, they were older and needed more to make a good impression in society. And, the cousins were making every effort to impress their society.

Their latest efforts entailed the city's annual masquerade ball. They made the event sound so wonderful that Cindy began to dream about going herself. However, she knew, for her, it could only be a dream.

Then, one day when Cindy was home alone, a woman came to the door. Cindy told the woman that her aunt wasn't home, but the woman told her that it was she that the woman wanted to see. The woman told her she had been her mother's friend and that she was actually Cindy's God Mother. The woman's name was Faith Moon. She told Cindy:

It is my duty as God Mother to do things for you.
I bet that you want to attend the costume ball.
That is exactly what I am here to help you to do.
I've brought the dress I last wore to the ball.
And I have brought a golden mask for you.

To alter it to fit should be an easy task for you.
I have arranged for limited use of a limousine,
Now, after all the others leave, it'll come for you.
But, then, at twelve from the ball you will have to go.
These things were easily done just for you.
The hardest part is left to you.

Perhaps it will help you to follow this advice:
Let me a riddle now to you present.
What do we see as a reality
But it, indeed, is opposite of true?

The answer has a special meaning I give to you.
Most people think they are the center of the universe.
If you are wise, you won't be as they are.

A mirror is the answer to the riddle that I posed.
It will reverse all things it does reflect.
Left is right, right is left.

Make as the center of your world
Not the false image in the mirror you now see,
But make of it the person talking then with you
And know it will reflect most positively back on you.

By being wise, you will do better than a mirror can.
Wise people look beyond themselves.
Take now an interest in others to the ball.
Your wisdom will make you the fairest of them all!

So, Cindy went to the ball. She danced, had fun and listened to everyone, including a tall, dark stranger. It was almost midnight before he asked her to dance. He had been surrounded all evening with eligible women, in particular Cindy's cousins.

While they danced, Cindy learned that he had recently graduated law school and come to town to begin his practice. She shared Mother Moon's riddle with him.

She was enjoying dancing with him so much that she lost track of time. When the clock chimed she realized that the rental on the limousine soon would expire; so she ran out the door.

The young handsome lawyer was surprised and disappointed at her sudden departure. He hadn't even asked her name. He had to know the identity of the woman in the golden mask. So, the next day, he placed an ad in the paper offering a reward for the name of this lovely lass.

To his surprise, for days his office was filled with women wearing that same golden mask. Who would have thought that the mask could so easily be bought? For alas, he thought none of the women were the one he sought. But, how could he be sure?

Then he remembered her riddle. He began asking each woman to pose the riddle for him. Everyone tried, including the cousins. Even the aunt made her pitch. Finally, the three of them decided that they might as well let Cindy take a shot.

When she did, the young handsome lawyer titled her the Bell of the Ball and the Queen of His Heart. After that, he made sure that the aunt dealt with Cindy the way that her parents intended. By the time she graduated from college, his was the strongest law practices in the town, and they lived happily ever after.

Miss Hollywood

Once on a modern time, there was a high school drama teacher so aptly named Miss Hollywood. Miss Hollywood had never actually been to Hollywood, not even to California, but many people, especially her students, thought she had. The way in which she continually referenced behaviors of famous actors, usually calling them by their first names, easily justified this misconception.

The misconception among her students contributed to Miss Hollywood's popularity. However, there were other factors that drew students to her. She had a degree of natural beauty and considerable ability to enhance her natural features.

So, Miss Hollywood was a favorite among the students. And, although she wouldn't admit it, perhaps even to herself, Miss Hollywood had favorites also. Among them was Lilly Lochs, a bubbly student with flowing golden hair.

Miss Hollywood told herself that the reason she liked Lilly so much was that she had real talent for the stage. However, the talents that attracted Miss Hollywood's attention were those that set Lilly apart from the other students. Lilly loved to call attention to herself by misbehaving.

Miss Hollywood set out to help Lilly by improving her self-esteem. Miss Hollywood had entered her teaching career with the firm belief that the center of all discipline problems was a lack of self-esteem. Therefore, she went about setting up experiences where she could reward Lilly at every opportunity.

Contrary to Miss Hollywood's belief that she was improving Lilly's behavior by increasing her confidence in herself, Lilly was caught in the act of burglarizing the Bier's country estate. The Biers were not at home at the time, but their silent alarm alerted the police. They arrested Lochs.

Miss Hollywood was incensed that Lilly was arrested over what was basically a prank. She decided to mount a campaign in Lilly's behalf. She quickly found that she could not muster support for her campaign among her fellow teachers.

She, then, looked for another source of help. She remembered hearing about a woman named Faith Moon. Moon had a reputation for helping the helpless and so forth. So Miss Hollywood took her case to Mother Moon.

Faith listened to Miss Hollywood's presentation and then replied:

I am reminded of two killdeer guarding their small nest.
They make a ruckus even when there is no harm about.

The act of Lilly Lochs was not a prank.
Official action needs now to be taken and will be.
She needs to learn that breaking laws has consequences.

Her actions in the past may have been to get seen.
No doubt she wants attention even when it's bad.
She does need to be taught how to gain attention in positive ways.

Rewards need to be based on
Substantive acts, not sinecures.

For ultimately good esteem for self comes from within.
Receiving false rewards gives people doubts both in the system
and themselves.

Miss Hollywood left Faith Moon still in search of support for her campaign. She failed to find it.

Lilly Lochs was lucky. She was given work probation where she was assigned to help the Biers. During that probation she felt a sense of accomplishment in the tasks she completed. She also met and became friends with the Biers' son.

Ariel

Once on a modern time, the Mayor of the town had only one child, a daughter named Ariel. Her mother died when she was fifteen.

Ariel was, of course, the pride of her father's life and rightly so. Ariel was an attractive girl and very athletic. She excelled in track and basketball, but her greatest talent was swimming. Year after year, she won gold medals in more than one event in local competitions.

When she entered high school, the swim coach encouraged her to try out for the Olympics. Her father resisted her participation. To him, she was too young, especially if she

were selected. She would be away from home for too long
a time. However, he did acquiesce, at least to the trials.
In these trials, the competition was much keener. Ariel did
not make the cut. However, she did impress the judges
enough that she was asked to accompany the team to the
Olympics to help the team and receive additional instruction.

Her father opposed her accepting the invitation. He didn't
see any honor in her being a gofer for the team. By the time
of the next Olympics she should be in college. By then, she
might no longer be interested in swimming. Mostly, he knew
the main reason he objected was that his daughter would be
away from home for many weeks. In the end, however, he
could not deny his daughter her desire to go.

Her experience as team assistant helped Ariel to be
a more intelligent and committed swimmer. During her
high school years she became even more competitive
winning many state and regional medals. Many universities
recruited her.

Of course, her father dreaded her leaving home to go
to college and hoped that she would select a school close
to home. He feared that she would select a west coast
university, so far from home.

Eventually, she chose a school in the D.C. area. She
liked the assistant coach who recruited her and the college
assured her an excellent education.

The spring of her second year, months before the
Olympic trials began, an event happened that changed the
course of her life. While on a study break, she went boating
with friends on the Potomac. A man from a nearby boat fell

into the water. It was obvious that he could not swim and was drowning. Immediately, Ariel dived in and pulled the man to safety.

The man was Japanese. He, Eroji, worked at the Japanese Embassy. He was a member of a rich and influential family. He was handsome, polite and charming. He insisted on showing his appreciation. Ariel, for the first time, learned the meaning of love.

She also knew from the depths of her soul that the relationship had two strong enemies. Her father, whose older brother was killed in World War II, harbored resentments against the Japanese. Also, her coach would not want any romantic distractions that would affect her training. Recognizing these strong forces did not prevent Ariel from responding positively to the young man's advances.

The assistant coach quickly saw the impact of Ariel's new relationship. Love for her young man rapidly drew her away from her swimming. The coach knew that he had to get her away from her Japanese.

Therefore, the coach developed a plan. He would persuade her father to let her go to a more swimming-directed program in California. With her as a prize, another program would award him a better job. It would be a win-win option for him.

On learning from the coach that his daughter was involved with a Japanese man, the Mayor was much distressed. The involvement was bad enough unto itself, but he also had to learn of it from someone else.

Once he calmed down sufficiently, the Mayor called his

daughter. The case turned out to be worse than the coach presented. Ariel told her father that swimming was no longer important to her and that Eroji and she were talking about spending their life together. Eroji wanted to meet her father and for her to visit Japan.

"Where would you live?" he asked.

"I will live with him wherever he lives. Father, you cannot deny me my destiny."

The Mayor was saddened by her words. He did not know what he could do. He couldn't force her to stay. To send her to California was anything but a solution. She would be unhappy with him and would be far from home at that. He didn't know how he would cope if she lived in Japan. He had lost Ariel's mother. Now it looked as if he was losing Ariel, too.

Over the next week, he went about his work without enthusiasm. Among his tasks was working with a committee to develop a community garden. Faith Moon was a prime mover on that committee. After a meeting, she mentioned to the Mayor that he didn't seem to be himself. So, he told her about Ariel's relationship with the Japanese, ending that he was likely to lose his daughter.

Mother Moon responded in a soft voice:

Do focus on what you have and have had,
Not on what you think you have lost.
You can't lose what you never had.
Do not dwell on your sense of loss.
Do not make of your love a barrier.
Be happy in your daughter's joy.

You cannot trap the spirit of your mermaid in a jar.
You must allow the birds to fly up in the sky.
You cannot tame the spirits of wild horses.
You must let her free spirit go.

You must let her free spirit now be free.
Don't keep your goldfish in a bowl.
The Japanese build ponds for their koi.

Prepare a feast and celebrate!
Continue to build on your life.
You never lose your daughter's love,
However, it you can destroy.

Start treasuring that which you have.
With her, traditions you have built.
She will take those with her.
And, with them, she will take the essence of your soul.

By treasuring the memories that your traditions give,
You make of all these memories a monument.

When you're together and when you're apart,
Your shared traditions will be monuments
That you together will continually visit even when you are apart.
So turn your memories into monuments.

The Mayor did not support the coach's plan to steal Ariel away. Ariel decided to visit Japan instead of participating in the Olympic games that next summer. After Ariel graduated, she and Eroji were married twice, once in the new community garden and again among the cherry petals of Kyoto. From their home, they enjoyed those fragrances from the cherry blossoms and lived happily ever after.

The Mayor did not see much of Ariel after her wedding, but still he felt close to her. He understood that all Japanese, like all Americans, are different,

When the community garden was well-established, he put a small statue of a mermaid at its entrance.

Judith Blue

Once on a modern time, Faith Moon knew
when she saw Judith Blue approaching, that
she wanted to talk about her younger son, Billy.
Judith's older son, Bob, now in his third year at the
university, had never been any problem. Billy had.

Mrs. Blue rushed to get through the conventional formalities and to Billy's problems. Billy had formed a band during his last year in high school. The band had early success in the area that year and the band decided to take it on the road. Billy had requested cash in lieu of financial support for his college education.

Judith Blue had vigorously opposed the idea, but her husband, Robert, said that Billy wasn't a little boy anymore. So, Billy, with his horn and his parent's cash, went off in search of fame and fortune.

As Mrs. Blue has learned, members of the band soon fell into disagreements and each went his separate way. Billy's funds permitted him to seek independent gigs only for so long. Now Billy was playing for contributions on street corners in a distant city. His situation there sounded grim.

Judith said, "I knew it would come to this! I knew it, I knew it!"

Faith Moon replied:

Now, do you want to be right or to help your son?
Your husband's call was right in letting him decide.
Your children aren't your children as the poet says.

You can't make key decisions for your children once they
        are mature.
You can only help them make the choices that are most right
        for them.
You can't prevent their walking the wrong path.
When they fail, you can only help them to learn from their
        mistakes.

Now you must be the calm, still pond
Reflecting the old weeping willow tree.
Do listen to your child as the deep pond
Reflects emotions of the tree.
And listen like the same pond hears
The plaintive coo of the deserted dove.

For only then can you help your child to see his route home.
You know you have provided him your love and values.
Have faith that those will enable him to find the right way home.

As she was on the way to that distant city, Mrs. Blue thought how much Mother Moon represented a model of the pond she described.

Soon thereafter, Billy returned home to ask for his parents' forgiveness. They met him at the bus station with open arms. That weekend the Blues threw a feast to celebrate Billy's return home.

Robert Blue

Once on a modern time, Robert Blue began to have doubts about his life and the decisions he had made. He had spent his life working hard. He built a farmer's supply business from scratch. He managed to provide for his wife and two sons, but he knew he had neglected too often his sons.

His older, Bob, was doing well at college, but his younger son, Bill, had decided instead of going to college to be a professional musician. Bill asked his parents to finance his band in lieu of sending him to college. Robert had acquiesced to his younger son's request; but alas, in less than one year's time, Bill had gone through all his money and was begging on the streets in a distant city.

Robert, who knew people in that city through his business travels, learned of his son's misfortunes. Really, for the first time in his life, Robert felt truly helpless. He had supported Bill's decision over his wife's objections. He didn't feel comfortable either openly going to fetch Bill back home or to do it clandestinely behind Mrs. Blue's back. Yet, he did feel that it was something he must do.

Then, to Robert's surprise, he learned that his son, of his own accord, was returning home. Robert ordered a feast be prepared for the weekend and met Bill when he got off the bus. Robert felt overwhelming joy.

However, Robert's happiness was short-lived. When Bob returned home from college that weekend and learned that a feast had been prepared for his wayward brother, Bob was furious.

Bob said to his father, "You never loved me. You never had any time for me all the years I was growing up. Still, I've done what a good son should. Unlike Billy who could never do anything but blow his horn. Now you're throwing a party for him. You've never done anything special for me."

Robert's feelings of profound doubts in his life's decisions crystallized as he watched his heir storm from the store that day. These feelings intensified into the next week as he continued his daily routine.

Bob returned to school and Bill came to work at the store. Robert worried that he had traded one son for the other. Then, as he watched Bill go through the paces, Robert began to fear that both were actually lost.

It was during that week that Faith Moon came to the store to buy some supplies for her spring garden. She was surprised to see Robert so dejected and inquired as to the reason.

Robert knew that his wife often confided in Faith Moon, but he never had. It wasn't in his nature to share his personal business with anyone. Then, until recently, he had never felt that he had personal problems. So, he decided to share with the good Faith Moon. She listened as he related the biting words of his older son and then she said:

I know that it was difficult to hear him say those things.
Perhaps he is like you: his thoughts were only of himself.
How often have you said to him, "We'll get together then...?"
His bad behavior helped you to see your own mistakes.

You should repent for your past sins.
Yet, you need not repent all aspects of your life.
And ask forgiveness both from Bob and from yourself,
But ask forgiveness only for the sins you did commit.

On close inspection, nature seems composed with many mistakes.
The sapling blocked from the sun produces a mangled tree.
The spider weaves to the deformed branch producing asymmetric
lines.
Still, to our eyes, it all appears a beautiful landscape.

Your sin was not in celebrating in your son's return.
By celebrating the return of your son, who was prodigal,
You acted as the father in the parable as told by Jesus Christ.
You wronged the one but not in welcoming back the other son.
As you know, you neglected what you should not have.

All make mistakes.
Therein is not the heart of us.
Repent for your mistakes,
But see the threads of your life as a total weave.

Robert Blue felt better after his talk with Mother Moon. He knew that he had forgiven himself. He continued his day with a resolve to do better by his sons, both of his sons.

Bob Blue

Once on a modern time, Bob Blue remained angry but he went to worship services anyway. He felt he had been treated unfairly, to say the least. He had always done his best to be the model son and, indeed, a model for his younger brother, Billy.

In contrast, Billy had been allowed to do, and fairly much did, whatever he wanted. What Billy had always wanted to do was practice on that trumpet of his. To Bob's amazement, Billy got more attention from his parents than he did. Indeed, Bob felt that he got no attention from his dad despite his excellent grades throughout high school and now through three years of college.

Last year, when Billy announced that he wasn't going to college, Bob was not surprised. However, when his parents agreed to bankroll Billy's band, Bob was appalled. They gave Billy as much money, in one lump sum, as they had spent for his education over the past three years.

Now, Bob thought, little Billy was back, broke, his band a total failure, and his parents were treating him like some kind of conquering hero! Bob had told his dad how it made him feel, and his dad had apologized, if you could call it that! Billy was on the payroll at the family farming-supply business, enjoying all the benefits of living at home. Meanwhile Bob, himself, was off at college during the week learning how to actually contribute to the business. Bob just knew that he did more on the Saturdays when he worked there than Billy did all week.

On leaving the worship house, Bob saw Faith Moon. Her name had been mentioned by both his mother and father as being helpful in dealing with the situation of Billy's return. Bob felt like giving her a bit of his mind, but thought better of it. Doing so wouldn't improve the situation and it certainly wasn't going to change her. He also thought that basically she was a nice person, just as he was.

However, when she walked up to him, he changed his mind. Something about the way she was all smiles, like she had single-handedly solved all his family's problems, made him really want to put her in her place. So, he told her that he didn't know exactly what she had done but, whatever it was, she hadn't helped make the situation right at the Blues' house. An injustice had been affected against him and had not been corrected. In the future, perhaps it would be best if she just minded her own business!

To Bob's amazement, his speech seemed to have no impact on Mother Moon at all. He thought she might get offended, but she didn't seem so at all. If she accepted what he'd said, she might have apologized. She didn't appear ready to do that either. Instead, for the moment, she just stood there with that little smile of hers still on her face.

Finally, she spoke in a voice so soft that none of the others standing within feet of them could hear. Yet he heard her words so clearly:

You are an angry yet unfocused man,
Much like the golden carp that feeds on waste.
Consider your deep anger's rasping sore.
You feel neglected but you are much loved.

The rasping sore is not your brother's return.
It is your father's neglect, neglect seeded from love.
When you misplace a glove, do you not go in search of it?
When you find the one glove, its partner's value is increased.

It seems your Dad has now passed his cat's cradle on to you.
Today, you must decide how you want to reweave its threads
Your life has solid direction as his always had.
Can you forgive and season it with love?

Do not blame others for your problems now.
Instead forgive them and move forward with your life.
In order to grow past your father's past mistakes,
you must see them in your acts and forgive his sins.

Become as the black walnut as it shades the tender young redbud.
The tall black walnut does not envy the spring beauty of the
    smaller tree
Because the shade provider knows its seeds and wood are
    greatly prized.

Faith Moon was still smiling as she walked away that day, but Bob Blue was too stunned to notice. It was several minutes before he felt like he had come out of a spell. It was only when he was back at college that he knew he had forgiven his dad and then he repented for his anger.

Billy Blue

Once on a modern time, Billy Blue was not happy, but, as he told himself, at least he had a warm place to sleep and good food to eat. Billy worked at his father's farming-supply business. It was not what Billy wanted to do. Billy wanted to be a musician.

Last year, on graduating from high school, Billy negoti-
ated with his dad for money to permit his band to travel.
Instead of going to college as his brother, Bob, had done,
he was given the cost of the education to finance the tour.

During his senior year in high school, the band had done
well. They were all fine musicians, even if inexperienced.
They were booked somewhere in the county almost every
weekend and they all interacted so well together. All that
changed when they went on the road.

Gigs were much harder to come by. Their booking agent
seemed to have no time for them. Mostly, everyone seemed
to develop an ego. Within six months, Billy's money was
almost gone and one by one, so was his band. He found
himself far away from home playing for handouts, usually
sleeping on the street.

By the spring of that year, Billy was exhausted. Playing
all day and freezing at night, he was in a stupor. Then, one
day, standing before him he saw his mother. He took it as a
sign. He asked himself what he was doing. His father would
surely give him a job at the store and he could live on that
wage in grand style compared with his current state. The
vision of his mother just listened. He resolved to return
home and beg his father for a job. As soon as he saved
enough money for a bus ticket, he was on his way home.

To his surprise, his parents were at the bus station when
he arrived. How his father knew that he was coming, he
didn't know. He was just so happy when his dad embraced
him on departing the bus.

Indeed, his father threw him a welcome-home party
that weekend. Many of his friends, home for the weekend,
attended. So did his brother, Bob. Bob did not seem glad
to see him at all, but that did not dampen Billy's excitement

about being welcomed home so warmly.

That excitement faded over the ensuing weeks. Working at the store was a drag. More importantly, he knew he wasn't good at it. He wasn't good at remembering the inventory and he wasn't at all good with numbers either. Mostly he was preoccupied with thoughts of music. He would hear tunes in his head even as the customers were telling him about their pets or their fencing problems. He would be thinking about lyrics and words that rhymed with a brand name when he was checking out a customer.

Thoughts of rhyming couplets were exactly what was on his mind late one Friday when Faith Moon came to his counter. He was so deep in thought that he didn't even see her.

Her words entered his consciousness as if they were a continuation of the lyrics he was composing:

Somewhere beyond your rainbow
In the nigh, golden sky
There is a land you know as a dream
Where the music's no lullaby.

Your soul is in a desert land
Without the water of your horn.
You are too young to let your dreams
Depart from so little scorn.

Somewhere beyond your rainbow
Where golden corn does grow
There is a musical, cool land
Of grass, not desert sand.

The mockingbird wasn't born
With an array of songs
And his songs many a morn
Are only met with groans.

Now listen to the voices,
"Come blow your horn."
Your music has rhythm
The stage you do adorn.

Somewhere beyond your rainbow
Bluebirds nest.
Birds fly beyond the rainbow
All it takes is your best.

Billy rang up Mother Moon's purchases, but it was all like a dream. As a dream, it remained in his mind until years later when he was able to set some of her words to music. That weekend, Billy had a productive discussion with his brother. Bob proposed that Billy visit with some of the music faculty at the university. Perhaps there would be opportunities there for Billy to work full time and get music instruction part time.

The proposal developed over the summer into a concrete plan. The brothers rented an apartment together during that, Bob's senior, year. Bob came home every weekend to help manage the store. Billy played his music, mostly on the weekends, with a sharp classical trio with two of his fellow students.

Hans

Once on a modern time, a stranger came to town. Now it wasn't as if the town had never seen a stranger before. It had. However, it had never seen one like Hans.

Hans said he was German. There were Germans in the area. He didn't look anything like them. His skin was darker and he was lean. Somehow, that was enough to make some people not trust him.

He claimed to be an artist. That was different. The only artists anyone knew were teachers and students at the college, and he was not at the college.

Indeed, he didn't work anywhere. He did odd jobs now and again. In the summers, enough people trusted him to let him do yard work, paint houses or complete other outside jobs.

Soon after he arrived in town, he volunteered for the children's reading hour at the library. However, before long, the librarian had to ask him to stop. Too many parents refused to leave their children when he was there.

He was good with young people, though, and they seemed drawn to him. In the spring, the student committee asked him to help with decorating for the prom. The job called for building skills coupled with artistic ability. Hans had both.

The committee told him they couldn't pay him much, little more than enough to cover his expenses. Still, jobs for him had been few all winter, and he thought it would be good advertising. So, he put his full attention to the task.

His effort surpassed the committee's wildest expectation. Everyone said the decorations were the greatest that the school ever had. However, when Hans came to school on Monday to present his bill, he was told that the student committee had no authority to authorize his expenses.

Angry, Hans made quite a scene. He made threats that he really didn't mean and, probably, had little ability to accomplish. Nevertheless, the threats soon spread across the town. People, then, actually began to fear Hans.

The town's Mayor, feeling the need to take some action to protect the town's youth from Hans, decided to ask Faith Moon to talk with Hans. Faith Moon had helped the Mayor resolve problems in the past. He hoped that she might find a solution to this problem as well.

Thus, Mother Moon sought and found Hans. He lived in a hovel, but once inside, she was impressed. He had turned it into a combination studio-gallery. He had produced lovely and exciting pieces from what had previously been trash. Faith admired an ornate flute carved from a piece of driftwood. She even purchased a planter hewed from an old tree stump.

On her inquiry, Hans told her why he was angry with the school. Her face showed disgust while he was telling his story. When he finished, she replied:

The school unfairly treated you.
That's clear for me to see.
We must next find the best course to pursue
To make your case to the community.

Your anger may be justified.
But, idle threats do nothing good for you.
Our anger is good only for the energy
To help us to do what we need to do.

Your talent permits you to see the beauty in what others see
       as trash.
Even driftwood has much worth when touched by the
       artist's hand.
This principle we need to make most clear for others to see.

Like your art, we need an apt solution to produce,
So to remove the problem that exists today in the community.

The education board must honor your claim
And the commerce chamber must promote your work.
We need to use your energy for good
And, thus, allow the world to see your work.

True to her word, Mother Moon helped Hans to collect his pay from the Board of Education. The Chamber was forthcoming with a corner to show Hans' creations. Soon, the library also had a display, followed by one at the college.

The exhibition at the college drew a wide viewing. Among those who visited was a graduate of the college, who owned a gallery in New York. The offer to come to New York was too good for Hans to refuse. Thereafter, the town took pride in the German artist who once lived among them.

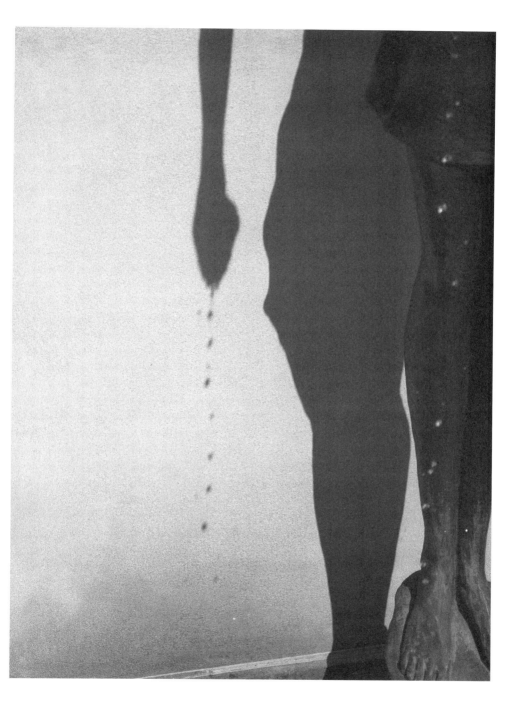

Barnum

Once on a modern time, Barnum lived a dull life. It had been an average life. He'd had no real problems, but no excitement either. He completed a degree in business. He worked for an insurance company and made enough money to live his average life.

Mostly, Barnum felt a need for romance. He had felt that way since he was in his teens. He'd had his share of dates during this time, but usually they involved dating a woman one time. They simply didn't find him interesting enough to see him again.

That is until he met Lola. Lola was the type of woman who never before had given Barnum a second look, much less a second date. Lola wasn't gorgeous but she was vivacious. She was full of energy and when she looked at a man, the man was happy. She looked at Barnum and his heart raced.

Barnum didn't know what Lola saw in him. All he knew was that when he was with her, all he could think about was wedding bells and white picket fences. When he wasn't with her, all he could think about was the next time he would see her.

Soon they were seeing each other every weekend. Barnum took her to the finest restaurants, the latest shows, the best clubs. It was so exciting. His life was no longer dull. Still, it was not the life he wanted. He wanted to marry Lola.

Anytime Barnum would approach anything close to the subject of marriage, Lola would redirect the conversation. However, on a moonlit night, Barnum was able to put the question before her.

She recoiled with a laugh, "Barnum, don't be silly. You know we're not serious. My real fellow is a ball player. He's away a lot, with training and games and all. When he makes it to the big leagues, he'll send for me. Until then, we'll just have fun, okay?"

Barnum could not get past the hurt he felt. He felt so used. As much as he wished he could, he knew he could never see Lola again.

Of course, Barnum's mood affected his work. No one liked seeing a salesman anyway, much less when he was in a bad mood. Then, into his office came one of his clients that he had never met. She had bought her policy from his predecessor. She had been in a minor accident. Her policy listed her as Faith Moon.

He processed her claim with his current lethargy. She asked him what was bothering him, and he, without understanding exactly why, told this complete stranger all about Lola and his broken heart. She listened to his story with no reaction save in her face, but Barnum knew she was understanding him. When he finished, Mother Moon said.

She did you wrong,
But you do yourself worse.
You dwell on that which can't be changed.
What you can't change, accept.

Some path besides the one of sorrow, you must walk.
You know the story about the boy without any shoes.
You have shoes and yet you don't walk.

You need to build a dam,
A watering spot to provide
For others' needs just to fulfill.
Companionship will then come to your side.

And, seek your mate among those most like you.
But look not first for that soul mate.
Help those without shoes and without any hope.
When you lose your sorrow in helping others reach their goal,
Your goal will be very close at hand.

First, Barnum sought to heed Mother Moon's advice by delivering meals to shut-ins. His mood improved immediately. A fellow volunteer told him that his help was really needed in working with area youth, especially those interested in business. He found that involvement most fulfilling.

It was in working with this youth business club that he met Bailey. Soon, Barnum saw how much like him she was. To his surprise, she was also attracted to him. They were married in the spring and lived happily ever after.

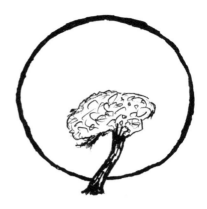

Joe

Once on a modern time, there lived a man named Joe. Joe was a good person. He prayed daily. His were prayers full of concern for others. Indeed, his hopes were primarily for the welfare of others.

When Joe did consider his personal desires, his principal thoughts were to marry a good woman and to raise a religious family. Joe conducted his personal life in a way as to be worthy of such a good woman.

When Joe first saw Mary, he saw the perfection of her body, and he decided that Mary was too attractive and, indeed, too popular for him. She was surrounded often by men.

However, when Mary spoke with Joe, and he looked into her eyes his heart filled with hope. As he listened to her, he believed that her perfection was more than physical.

Over time, Joe found more opportunities to discuss life's issues with Mary. The more discussions they had, the more Joe realized that he loved Mary and began to hope that Mary loved him.

In time, Joe found the courage to tell Mary something of the depths of his feelings for her. To his surprise and to his disappointment, she said, "Joe, as much as I've longed to hear those words, you must forget those feelings and forget me."

Joe steeled himself enough to ask why, but Mary shook her head and began to cry. Joe took her into his arms and he heard through her sobs, "Joe, I'm with child."

Joe did not know what to say. When Mary pulled back and ran away, Joe allowed her to flee.

Joe needed to talk to someone. One person he respected greatly was Mother Moon. Faith Moon listened to Joe and Joe felt better.

When Joe finished, the kindly old woman said:

Ask not perfection from another soul
For you cannot find it within yourself.

If you wait for a perfect one
Then either disappointment or distortion waits for you.

You must accept the imperfection that is her
Before you can accept it in yourself.
Thus is the heart of humanity.

The red male hawk will soar the skies
But the old buzzard soars still higher and stays longer in
           the clouds.
Yet, the old buzzard never will enjoy
The diet nor display the colors of sir hawk.

We all have our own strengths
And our own weaknesses.
Accept your faults and help others to find their strengths.
Therein we find our happiness.

Joe left knowing what he needed to do. Mary and Joe were soon married. That spring they had a lovely baby son.

John Spratt

Once on a modern time, John Spratt and his wife lived alone. The Spratts were not religious people. They didn't regularly attend worship services. However, when Martha decided she wanted to do so, there was little doubt that they would. John wasn't likely to stand up successfully to her demand. He never had. Whatever Martha wanted, John acquiesced. Provided, of course, that it was in his power to do so.

You see Martha had what the intellectual community called an aggressive personality. John was nominally a member of the intellectual community. He knew Martha's nature. He had known it when he married her. John had a submissive personality. John recognized that theirs would be labeled a complementary relationship.

Martha's late father had been Dean when he hired John as Instructor of English. John was working on his dissertation at the time. Once John married Martha, he stopped working on the dissertation. He received tenure at the college anyway. He, but not Martha, had resigned himself to being an Instructor of English forever.

He had not, however, resigned himself to obeying Martha completely. They had a younger couple over for dinner that Friday night. When Martha announced that they were going to worship that weekend, his resolve stiffened.

"It's not a holy day!" said he.

"It is to me!" She said and turned to their guest, "It's our baby's birthday."

The guests were agape. "I didn't know you had a child!" they said in unison.

"We don't," said John and changed the subject.

Of course, John's denial only spurred Martha to greater dominance of John throughout the evening. Eventually, he screamed at her, "Stop it! I can't take it anymore!"

She looked him straight in the eyes and calmly said, "You can take it. You married me for it."

So they went to worship that weekend. However, John's resistance continued. He didn't do as she wished as quickly as she desired. Their bickering continued before the service, at times during it, disturbing the worship, and as they were leaving the building.

Outside, they were approached by a woman who they recognized as a friend of Martha's father, a Faith Moon. She said to them:

You really need to get help!
A marriage shouldn't be like a bramble bush!
Nor should it be like boulders leaning one on one.

The husband is submissive and aggressive is the wife.
Assertive you both need to be.
For neither of you listen; you just talk.
Instead of focusing on what you want,
You need together to consider your joint goals.

Yes, let your marriage be as one reflected by the cypress and the
      oak, separate and strong.
Yet, let your leaves unite to provide shade for good mother earth
      who nourishes us all.
Together, She and you can nurture seeds of your relationship
      whatever they will soon produce.

Yes, eat from your own plate,
But do be mindful of the other's plate to tend.
For only then will yours be a complete relationship,
And only then will your meal be one of togetherness!

The Spratts did not listen to Mother Moon. They did not change their behavior toward each other. Yet, who is to know? Perhaps they lived happily ever after.

Grace Terra

Once on a modern time, a few individuals noticed that Faith Moon wasn't well. However, it was only when Faith stopped attending worship services that most people noticed.

Soon thereafter, word spread across the town that she was seriously ill. Her daughter, Grace, had come to town to be with her mother. She was admitted to the hospital. Mr. Thomas, the neighborhood grocer, who was financially well to do, offered to sponsor a trip for Mother Moon to see the best specialist available. Mother Moon, it was rumored, graciously refused his offer.

Then, Mother Moon was moved from the hospital to her home, the local doctors having done all for her that they could. A vigil of neighbors helped Grace to see to her mother's needs.

Several days passed before word went out beckoning people to come to the worship house. Grace had a statement from her mother. The house was filled to overflowing.

Everyone could hear her mother's calm tones in Grace's voice. After thanking everyone for coming, she read the following statement from her mother:

Don't weep for me, those whom I love
And who for me have often shared your love.
Love, for life's capstone, is the best.
That is why I'm now ready to rest.

Life has been good to me.
I have not traveled far
Nor published anything.
My light, still, hasn't been in a jar.

God has been good to me.
The God, whom we do see
In nature, calls to me.
Sad you should not be.

In nature's life plan overall
Death is a necessary thing
Even as the decay of fall
Provides the beauty come the spring.

As a seed planter after a brush fire
I always tried to live my life.
Please honor me in all your memories
By taking those seeds into your lives.

Don't weep too long for me.
Don't pity yourself at my loss.
And, don't be mad at me once I am dead.
Take hope in knowing others you can help.

Thanks for allowing me to be part of your life.

Life is for you to live.
Please go live it!

Grace arranged the affairs of her mother's estate. Faith Moon did not own much. What possessions she had were parceled out to members of the community. Everyone who received an item felt special. Faith's house sold quickly and Grace returned to her family.

Grace never returned. However, everyone remembered her and they strove to live their lives as Faith had requested.

The people enjoyed the community garden that Faith had helped to start. Indeed, in what many called a miracle, in an area of the garden that had been most troublesome, the next Easter a lily bloomed.

So, many in the town believed that the spirit of Mother Moon still watched over them and they tended their garden happily ever after.

Jill and Jack

Once on a modern time, Jack and Jill went off to war. Except for the war, they would have never fallen in love. They had never even spoken to each other in all their years living in the same town. They had much in common, factors that led each to join the Guard. However, beyond their gender, there was one major difference between them: One had creamy dark skin, the other's was rosy pale.

The war brought them together and simplified their relationship, but they knew their relationship would be impossible back home. Jack's father would turn over in his grave if he knew Jack was even being friendly to Jill. Jill's father might not even open their front door for Jack.

Jack and Jill avoided discussing the future. Staying alive occupied most of their time; they treasured their moments together. Yet, the time came when they were forced to discuss the return home.

Jack's mother rejoiced when she read the letter confirming that his unit was returning home. Her joy was dampened, however, as she continued to read. She could not believe her eyes. How could he be engaged to Jill? How would he deal with his old friends? How would he cope? How would she?

She needed to talk with someone she could trust. She thought of a friend from worship, a woman everyone called Sister Terra.

Grace Terra listened to Jack's mother and Sister Terra clearly understood. When Jack's mother finished, the kindly woman said:

Love always does provide pure pleasure to the just,
But it must sometimes bring real pain.

Love needs acceptance by the ones we value.
When they do not support our love, it hurts that love.
It can be for the best, but often it's not,
Like Romeo and Juliet.

A love between two souls can bring them bliss,
But still the love requires a nourishment
Provided by acceptance in our garden of society.

Consider gardens you have seen on earth.
How beautiful they are in colors all array!
Why do you want the garden that is God's to be so different?

Jack's mother wasn't sure that she understood all that she heard, but her soul knew. It had known all along how much she loved her son.

When Jack received his mother's letter, he was pleased. Her acceptance of Jill would make a difference. It did, but you know that for Jack and Jill to live happily ever after they needed the support of so many other people.

THE END